Broken and Blended:
Love's Alchemy

Broken and Blended:
Love's Alchemy

Poems by

Harry Moore

© 2021 Harry Moore. All rights reserved.
This material may not be reproduced in any form, published,
reprinted, recorded, performed, broadcast,
rewritten or redistributed without
the explicit permission of Harry Moore.
All such actions are strictly prohibited by law.

Cover photograph by Harry Moore
Cover design by Shay Culligan

ISBN: 978-1-954353-66-4

Kelsay Books
502 South 1040 East, A-119
American Fork, Utah, 84003

For Cassandra, who taught me
yours and mine
are ours

"To everything there is a season…a time to break down
and a time to build up…a time to mourn, and a time
to dance…a time to keep silence, and a time to speak…"
—Ecclesiastes 3:1-7, KJV

Acknowledgments

My thanks to the following publications, in which some poems in this collection first appeared:

Alabama Literary Review: "License My Roving Hands," "A Summer's Day," "Time's Fool"
Bearing the Farm Away (Kelsay Books, 2018): "Moving On"
Beyond Paradise: The Unweeded Garden (Main Street Rag, 2020): "Decisions and Revisions"
Blue Unicorn: "Absence"
Cullman Tribune: "Packing Up"
Elk River Review: "Long Distance"
English Journal: "GP's Wife Does National Boards" Copyright 2003 by NCTE. Used by permission.
Main Street Rag: "To Your Health," "Sure Thing"
POEM: "As You Like It," "Ushering at Easter"
Poets' Choice: "Darwin Chuckles," "The Stapler," "Packing Up"
Pudding Magazine: "Controlling the Narrative"
Retreat: A Way Forward (Finishing Line Press, 2017): "Turn, Turn, Turn," "Eros," "Forbidding Mourning"
SCETC Journal: "Decisions and Revisions," "Anniversary"
Ship of Fools: "Breaking Up," "Eros"
South Carolina Review: "Valediction"
Time's Fool: Love Poems (Mule on a Ferris Wheel Press, 2014): "Long Distance," "Time's Fool," "License My Roving Hands," "GP's Wife Does National Boards," "As You Like It," "A Summer's Day," "Youngest," "Ushering at Easter"
What He Would Call Them (Finishing Line Press, 2013): "Valediction"

Etymologies that appear as epigraphs are from *Webster's New World College Dictionary,* 4th ed. Echoes of English and American writers I taught in the classroom for four decades are of course deliberate—especially Spenser, Shakespeare, and Donne, but also Keats, Frost, Eliot, and Deborah Pope.

Contents

Part I: A Time to Speak

Controlling the Narrative	17
An Old Tale	19

Part II: A Time to Mourn

Breaking Up	23
Some Say Love	24
On the Run (I)	26
On the Run (II)	27
Moving On	28
Forgetting	29
Long Distance	30
Time's Fool	32
Two Planets	33
The Stapler	34

Part III: A Time to Embrace

Valediction	37
It's My Story	39
Decisions and Revisions	40
Turn, Turn, Turn	41
Eros	42
Anniversary	43
License My Roving Hands	44
Forbidding Mourning	45

Part IV: A Time to Heal

A Summer's Day	49
Flashback	51
Youngest	52

The Sentence	53
Ushering at Easter or GP Notices His Stepdaughter	54
Not-Father	56
Home Again	58
A Place of His Own	59
The Eagle	61

Part V: A Time to Build Up

The Royal Family	65
Actually	67
Breakfast at the Beach	68
The Call	70
Hands	72
Consider Lillie	74
Jonah	76
Sophie	78

Part VI: A Time to Dance

GP's Wife Does National Boards	83
As You Like It or GP Goes to London with His Wife	84
Darwin Chuckles or GP Studies Natural Selection	86
About Time	88
Probably Not or The Tangled Art of Connubial Meta-Messages	89
Absence	90
An Evening	91
This Only	92
Aiding and Abetting	93

Part VII: A Time for Peace

Packing Up	97
All Things New	98
To Your Health	100
A Way Forward	102
Sure Thing	104

Part I: A Time to Speak

Controlling the Narrative

> < L *narrare,* to tell < IE *ĝnoro-,*
> base **ĝen-,* to know

We must be able to say what
happened,
               the clever bank heist;
the vacation fiasco, Jim tumbling
into the lake; the bloody horror
of children shot on some campus,
how the deranged shooter arrived
at this moment; how Jack and Sue's
marriage teetered, collapsed; the way
the glacier slid south on its own
melting; how natives picked their
way across the narrow strait and
dropped arrowheads in the field
our father plowed; how wandering
Odysseus found his way back.

There's justice, of course, solemn
witness to the facts, making people
pay for malice or negligence; and
humor, the incongruous twist even
preachers laugh at; and there's catharsis,
where saying the soldiers' wild slaughter
drags the inner demon from the dark.

But deepest of all, the familiar shape,
arc of the action, the way character
and circumstance converge, lovers
cling, enemies clash like a world of
molecules that won't bond.
                     In the story's
bend and flow, the voice's cadence,

the deft move of a woman's hand
as she tucks hair behind her ear and
laughs—we trace the curve of our
lives, the jagged line we take
through time. This is how we *know*.

An Old Tale

> < OE *talu,* speech, number
> < IE base **del-,* to aim, reckon,
>   trick

It was the speech that got her,
the talk, his dry scaly skin
brushing her hand and bare hip
as he pointed to the shiny fruit.

She knew what to eat and what
not and what creatures cavorted
and tumbled in play, but this one
chatted her up and offered dinner.

It was magic, he said, his eyes
dropping to her chest, the tongue
licking rapidly in all directions.
He'd dabbled in science and

philosophy and knew the trees.
Maybe there was more than she'd
been told, snipping shrubs and
lounging on unending holiday,

maybe some replanting and cross-
breeding, her gaze wandering beyond
the wall to blue sky and tall gathering
cumulus clouds to the west. He was

clever, for sure. He'd help her learn,
he said, know what to do, make her
count for something, his eyes raking
her torso before glancing away.

Trembling at how his words raised
a shimmering world beyond the world
she knew, an open vista she might
walk, command she might take,

she leaned into him, and reached
for the apple.

Part II: A Time to Mourn

Breaking Up

One day as I watched her my wife
disappeared went blank and clear as
a washed windowpane through which
I could see the painting of Christina
reaching out on the wall behind her
but that disappeared too and the wall
too disappeared before my eyes
like fog clearing or ice melting and there
as plain as day was our slate gray
Honda Civic with the small dent just front
of the left door until it too vanished
and the cement carport and the green
bermuda grass beyond and the maple
with the diseased hump and Mrs. Dinsmore's
red brick house next door and the white
clouds and blue sky the pale shell
of a moon in daytime all disappeared
as if a magician waved his wand. I saw
right through the dining room chairs
my little boy and the universe. I might
have felt for a stool I suppose instead
I ran weeping into the light falling heavily
once or twice on the lumpy ground
I could not see.

Some Say Love

> *"Such men are dangerous; they think too much."*
> —Shakespeare, *Julius Caesar*

She said she knew he was the one
the day he first walked in, tall
and straight and high of mind,
with college and a job, hardly one
to bend beneath a weight or wind.
She liked the way he said her name
and how he wore a coat and tie.
A vista opened up where
handsome horses pulled her coach
and she might have her dream.
And so she stood in church and
pledged undying love, her flame
and his condensed into a candle.

She found in him a shelter where
ancient hurts might heal and love
could never look away—a house
to show her worth, the days and years
her frugal parents spent on her,
their only daughter.

She said she knew that he would leave
when first he told his past, a promise
tossed like last year's hat, a party glass
gone dry. How could she trust
the outstretched hand? And so
they bled when ripped apart, angry
at their story's bitter turn, Cinderella
shoeless and in rags, ever-after
up in smoke.

How could she see his mantle
was borrowed from his father,
the knowing air, the certain word,
tilting fearless toward truth and right?
How could she know a boy
was in the saddle, whose lean
and errant eye searched every room
for damsels he might dream about?

On the Run (I)

On the asphalt track each Nike stride
grinds the scattered sand, jarring
muscle, bone, and brain, releasing

into July heat, step by step, a weight
of classroom duties, custody struggles,
shattered vows, and stacks of unpaid bills.

I pump my arms and keep the steady beat,
pressing past dark cedars and puffy clouds
toward some distant rest. A breeze stirs

at the turn, and odor of fresh-cut grass
rides the air with muffled shouts
from tennis courts. I spit dryly

to one side. In the jolt of every step,
the ooze and drip of sweat like seeping
memory, and my growing gasps for air,

I do not think
I am.

On the Run (II)

To the tall man in gray shorts
who circles the track by Southside School
in summer heat till he bends gulping air,

I pose the question of what
he is running from or for. What
fury shrieks behind him, what

Calypso leads him on? What
could this endless plodding be
but quest or flight?

Moving On

"...be one...on whom nothing is lost."
—Henry James, *The Art of Fiction*

You'll get *past* this, they say, as if grief
were a dangerous stretch of road, a canyon
where ambush might occur. Others say,

you'll get *through* it, loss being a fog or
jungle I can't see the other side of.
Impatient ones say, Get *over* it already,

as if I have only to climb my way across
a fence or mountain. But I don't think so.
The pain, the guilt, heavy thoughts at 3:00 a.m.

have grown familiar. They sink roots in my flesh,
grip my bones. They ride my pulsing blood.
I've found words for the hurt, charmed it,

making it sway like a cobra to my music.
It hammers away in a secret shop. Even
when I move on, the words go with me.

Forgetting

*Some nerves
time does not touch
taut strings
singing quietly
with old regrets.*

The happy times are hardest to forget:
how she lost herself in laughter
when he dropped a sunglass lens and walked
with pirate's patch in half-dim state
across the K-Mart parking lot, or when
the strange dog outside the sliding doors
squatted straining, facing them, his
intent and nervous gaze meeting theirs
in a moment's frame, or the love
they made that summer before
their son was born.

*Beneath his coat
he kept a flask of grief
from which he sipped
furtively.*

Painful times cut deep, fabric ripped,
cars smashed, stinging words flung
at the face, a wooden clinging
to what's dead. But closets grow
new fashions, scars fade, new actors
play familiar roles. Laughter
is the last to go, echoing still
in rooms we moved away from
years ago.

Long Distance

In the courtyard below my third-floor office
ash trees shade yellow in October sun.
Beyond the trees cars on I-65
whir and grind southward.

In the city of sluggers, I think of the plastic bat
you swung in our back yard ten years ago
and of the ash tree you climbed one summer day.
You were a sturdy five then
bold, husky, strong, driving
old tennis balls past me to the chain link fence
beyond the strawberry patch where
you and your friend ate the berries green,
but stranded on a limb five feet high
you cried help till I lifted you down
to solid ground.

Now at six feet one, a hundred ninety pounds
you play the trombone, study chemistry
and geometry, collect baseball cards and comics,
draw Ivan the Terrible, talk of archaeology
and of your dead grandfather
in pastures and woods where he led you.
You eat sandwiches as most people eat cookies
in three bites and you
punish a skateboard like Cyclops on a Volkswagen.

Your calls are frequent now.
Where would you go to school if you lived with me,
and how's the cat, the deepening casual voice
masking the child's urgency.

Beyond the ash trees yellowing in October sun
cars on I-65 whir and grind southward.
Once more I must decide
if I will come and get you.

Time's Fool

"Daddy?" she said, her cell phone voice
rising toward some question,
"We're getting married. Michael's
taking off Thanksgiving and we're
going to St. Simon's. You can
have a reception for us later, and
Mom can too."

She didn't say she missed me
when I left, the Golden Books we read
when she was two, songs we sang, or
waffles we two made while others slept
or that weekend roads were long and
houses far. She didn't say she needed me
with nouns and numbers and thunderstorms
that shook her sleep. She didn't ask
how we who bore her could not speak,
why in our years apart we built no bridge
a child might walk, no place
a girl might marry.

In the tape she sends of palm trees
and marbled seaside houses,
they stand outside before a man
in black robe, who calls them by their names,
wind scuffing the hidden mike and blowing
her dark hair. When she pledges lifelong love,
through riches, hunger, health, and time's slow
change, her voice trembles, her eyes glisten,
and I weep.

Two Planets

We circle her in separate orbits,
worlds apart—the auburn hair,
the steady wide-set eyes bluer
than our green, the sturdy shoulders—
we who loved each other once
and cradled her mother.

Mimi is Earth to her sun, feeds her
lunch, puts balm on bruises, says
which dress is best to wear. I am
Granddaddy, like Jupiter unwavering but far,
relishing the small voice on the phone
Thank you for the book, the firm hug
on rare visits, the invite to the playground,
chosen escort for the walk to school.

We two meet in her, a common center,
though our paths must never cross,
the bed we warmed for our daughter
now an ice age past. Will she draw us
from such remote and settled courses
with frank voice and open smile, or
will even she lack grace to break us
from our distant heart-locked ways?

The Stapler

Left decades past by an ex-wife who
took cars, furniture, china, children,

it is a rickety assemblage of plastic
and thin metal, its slender staples

routinely jamming, hanging, bending,
bristling on thick packets. Even so,

it holds together in a thousand files
most of what I think and need—poems,

teaching notes, Sunday school lessons,
travel ads, hotel confirmations, flight

plans, eulogy notes for friends. Why
do I reach for it instead of the bright

sturdy model that with a clean click
drives strong metal through ten pages

just where the arrow says? What does
it mean that I nurse along time's longest

possible arc this frail connector, pressing,
aligning, straightening, not ready to admit

it is coming apart?

Part III: A Time to Embrace

Valediction

She did not come all week when
at the rustle of clothes I glanced
at the door hoping to see her there
knocking lightly as she pushed forward,
flushing as she met my eye and smiled,
sitting casually before the desk
strewn with papers.

One time she said, "I need comfort;
I made 73 on an economics test,"
as if Adam Smith's third law said
she must not come without a reason.

And then today she came.
There were the brown eyes,
high cheekbones, taut and
lightly freckled, the short dark hair
tumbling toward her brow,
the upper lip lifted slightly
hinting of bemusement,
the slender body, inevitable jeans,
sweater, the easy gait.

Today was different, though,
no blush or nervous manner,
no studied nonchalance,
no apologetic edge when she said,
"I finally made an A." We talked
of houses, school, children, wasps
as before, but she didn't run her fingers through her hair,
and the eyes were steady but ungiving.

When she said, "It's about class time, I just thought
I'd tell you about my test,"
there was the deadly sense she meant it,
as if someone said, "Here's the five dollars I owe."

And now I must wonder if that old cave
I found in a red gully once
ever held anything more than mice and night birds
and the play money I buried there.

It's My Story

< history < Gr *eidenai,* to know
< IE base, **weid-* to see, know
> WISE

It starts with facts, this or that place,
a farm, bare toes wiggling in cool
May soil, who else was there, the pine-
paneled pulpit, Nelson Street, Woodland.

It winds through time, like a village's
growth before the storm—a lovers' tryst,
how he was fond of her, fonder than
any right he had, like a flood, perhaps,
or bull's-eye asteroid slamming Earth,
complication of the plot,
                        mounting suspense,
other places, times, two years of grinding
indecision, the pendulum poised like a
scimitar to cut away the past.
                        Then the pieces,
how they fit or don't in the new puzzle,
everything re-arranged, radiation after
the blast, children ferried between houses
on weekends, siblings bonding like the
edges of a wound, cleaned, dressed, till
only a pale scar remains.
                        The pattern
comes clear, how atoms bounce and connect,
everything dovetails, ripples merging like
choreographed fireworks in the night sky,
a crescendo,
                        the way she
laughed nervously and left to get her son,
the stream having forked, to see now how
everything hung on a word.

Decisions and Revisions

< L *de-,* off, from
+ *caedere,* to cut down, kill

Choices aren't easy
tasting, testing
but if that were all
life were a feast
apple or apricot Susan or Mary
taking on cargo packing the hold
ever wandering down new roads
slicing exotic melons
but alas one road
walked is another left
and we must sigh ages hence
decide   cut off   kill
what we don't choose
else the boat sinks
of fond hopes and
uncut phrases.

Turn, Turn, Turn

Choked and paralyzed for months,
pros and cons weighed by the pound

until beneath their balanced crush
he could not move. Every advance

canceled by retreat, inching forward
like a cosmic sloth, tectonic shift across

centuries. Ponderous mood swings,
Lady Fortune's wheel at high joy

already grinding toward regret and doubt.
Gazing at the lake's reflective surface,

sketching the face. An LP record hung
in the same scratchy groove till the needle

lurches sideways to a whole new song.

Eros

Love is a flood we catch
as we can. We bathe friends
in it, parents, children, sweethearts
naked in bed, splash it on dogs that
lick our hands, douse colleagues at work,
neighbors, people on our pew at church,
spray redbirds, mountain pines, blue sky,
stars at night, soak strawberries and poems
that swell with longing.

                      In it we swim, dive
to lung-bursting depths, exulting
in weightless dance. On it we launch ships
and float our bottled words. With it
we slake deepest thirst.

                      Without it,
Earth shrivels to dry sand, our body
is a valley of bones, all beauty mere
sticks, and every day is exile.

We always pray for wet—buds, blossoms,
breasts, showers, overflowing tubs, kisses,
hugs, puddles, drinks, laughter, kind deeds,
comfort, trust, hope, and, if we are lucky,
full tide under a beaming sun.

Anniversary

Twelve is the perfect one,
you know. Twelve books
make an epic, twelve
months a year, twelve days
make Christmas, twelve gates
open Paradise. And
twelve years make a marriage so deep
it dreams in your sleeping hand
on my pillow.

License My Roving Hands

Watching *Law and Order* reruns
from the worn loveseat our daughter gave us,
you lean forward, my cue to rub your neck
and back, kneading tight muscles, pressing
thumbs beside the spine, releasing a day
of early church, Sunday dinner, two children,
four grandchildren, your mother, and
deep planning for the beach. That hurts,
you say, when I squeeze your tender
shoulders, remembering how firm
and smooth and tan they were that night
three decades past when first I watched
your shirt drop away. Finally tissue
and tendon go soft, and you lean into
my pressing fingers, saying it feels good
and offering me a bite of chocolate
Weight Watchers' bar.

When I pat you saying that's all,
you lean against me, resting
snug beneath my arm. On TV,
the news at ten parades a troubled world.
Tomorrow I do *Beowulf* at 8:00 and
you teach Olivia words and drop
my shirts for cleaning. But now we sit,
your hair against my cheek, my hand
lightly on your hip, our little sunroom den
an everywhere.

Forbidding Mourning

Our calls that fall were frequent, only
across town but over a large chasm
of guilt and uncertainty, desperate tether
to a joy so new we couldn't know it
would last. Absence measured in minutes,
hours, threatening to explode into miles
too far to travel.

Four decades later, we are half a continent
apart, our clocks on different hours, for
a month, but your calls to the house phone
outside my door are calm, details of our
common life washing over us in quiet relief:
your mom came for lunch, you paid the plumber
and cleaning lady, the dog got out, our daughter
did church with you, you got your hair cut,
you miss me, you'll be in Natchez next week.
My exotic retreat merging seamlessly:
I walked the foothills today, saw deer, hawks,
and magpie, ate frozen pasta as you suggested,
worked hours from old journals, went with
the group to a rodeo, had beers at the Mint Bar,
can't wait to see you in Denver.

No need to weep or worry. Once hot as a
welder's arc, now tempered to all weathers.

Part IV: A Time to Heal

A Summer's Day

High in the La Platas, by spruce and fir,
my son shows me relics of the Lucky Moon Mine:
tan-colored tailings, like sawdust, rusted
iron bucket, corroded tin roof
from a collapsed cabin, and a growing
cover of currant bushes. In August sun,
he waves toward distant mountain rims,
ribbons of switchback road, sheer slopes
down which he boarded last winter.
Fingering rocks, he speaks of glaciers,
granite, limestone, fault lines
up which the molten metal surged.
Behind us, thunder jolts the earth.

When he was four, he piled flint and sandstone
by my mother's door, salvage
from a gravel road we walked.
She left them there for weeks, she said.

I've fled my Eastern classroom where language
is my trade, he his kitchen-concrete shop.
We're out for alpine air, chasing lost years.
I climb the slope, snapping cheap pictures,
naming phlox and cinquefoil, while far below
he probes the earth, kneeling, peering,
tossing, gathering rocks. With loaded arms,
he yells we'd better get to the jeep
or he will break it down.

At the treeline a hailstorm hits,
marble ice pinging the hood,
drumming the canvas top, filling
wood and ruts till we bounce and slide

laughing down slopes, through sharp turns
of the ancient road. All around us,
beneath the ghostly aspens, the ground
is white, like some winter world
where time has stopped.

Flashback

Sunday night. Phone rings. Long-grown son's
Western-state number flashes on the screen

where we watch *Downton Abbey*. He will want
Facetime, with Jonah and Sophie tossing blocks,

climbing, splashing in the bath, saying hi and
turning to their world. "Not on Sunday night!"

my wife of thirty years says. "Not now!" adding,
"He must have the kids on his own."

Flashback thirty-five years: a black dial-up
wall phone rings in the seedy apartment

I've moved to. "I need you over here!"
his panicked five-year-old voice cries, searing

its way into bone and brain.
                              Not this time.
"Hey, Son," I say, awaiting his rapid "Hey, Dad,"

and the easy slide into small talk about work,
snow, the kids, his beautiful mountain valley.

Youngest

Tall behind the lectern, she marched firmly
through the script, her voice bumpy,
then sure, across the graduation crowd.
She spoke of hope, ambition, gratitude,

familiar words she had years to unpack.
She always aimed to please, heaping A's
in our laps, second best in her class, playing
flute for her brother's drama. Her parents

might be worlds apart, but she would
love them both. Did the thunder she feared,
locked doors and elevator cars she fled,
reflect the world we made for her, walls

on every hand? Is this what gave her strength
beneath the ready smile, behind the tears
that rose when she disappointed? She found
a ledge of no retreat, a place where courage grew.

Now she runs to keep fit—mother, wife, daughter,
teacher—tender with shy or willful children who
shout or beg for her to look. Over biscuit crumbs
and jelly smears, she speaks softly to her daughter,

laughing at her dashed-off art, the woman
with a flip hair-do, her careless air of knowing
who she is. On the sofa, they collapse
into tickling and giggles. Each day's plan—

school, play, dance, tennis—guards Lillie's world,
its charted lines drawn deeply in the sand.

The Sentence

My daughter's fragmented e-mail phrases
say husband, teenager, and twenty
third-graders keep her running, she will
call this weekend, catch up.

            ***

Exhilarated with broad air, my release
from walls too close for breath when she
was two, how could I feel confinement

when the judge's gavel hammered us apart—
know I was leaving her behind? How could I
see that she would not remember our days

and nights in the same house, recalling
only weekend journeys to an odd street,
another mother, siblings appearing like

instant oatmeal? How could I miss how much
she meant to please—how phone calls, letters,
words led her on till she landed behind a lectern?

How could I know how often, at 40, she
would toss me catch-up calls, e-mails, pictures—
and how she never signs off with love

merely flung in my direction, but always in
a full sentence, three words marching forward,
subject, verb, object, righting our world,
her place in it, and mine.

Ushering at Easter
or
GP Notices His Stepdaughter

Lilies burst from ends of pews marking
the way the cross moves to the altar
and the tall bright window where St. John
writes gospel in his blue book.
As trumpets rise toward dark roofbeams,
hull of my ship these thirty years,
I see my daughter across the crowded church,
hair gone darker now, arms brown
from weeks of soccer sun, her form slight
in the straight frock, standing
between her daughters, now shoulder high.

She was oldest of the four
in our mix and match, already ten
when we met, shy, running fast,
fighting for her brother, smiling
when I caught her eye.

Steady as the clock that woke her
every day for school, she kept quiet
when voices roared. She was *pisces,*
I a *virgo* in a house of lions.
In broken French, my minor key,
we tossed words like keep-away
above the family's head. *Pas-pere*
she called me, childhood joke
as deep as blood.

Driving the red Datsun, she crashed
on geometry's hard proofs, fleeing
to her father's country house one term.
Later, north of childhood and college,
she drove nights to us through rain,
infant and toddler like loads of nectar
on the homeward flight.

After church, when children crowd
her mother's tiny kitchen, jostling
for grapes or ice cream,
she'll stand beside the glowing heater
just outside the tug and push.
Across the room, we will smile,
glad for laughter, food, casual talk,
hearts grown firm with years.

Not-Father

It was a stretch, we knew,
this splashing in the shallows
of a new and strange language,

a riff for a melody we were
making up on the fly,
                              but
the logic was impeccable. If *pas*
was *step,* a pacing in the new
house we were milling about in,

and if *père* of course was *father,*
the one finding his way who must
somehow be the guide, then it
followed as inexorably as any
algebra equation ever moved
that *Pas-Père* was my role.
                                And
if—ah, yes, if—with laughter
from the wings as we played
our parts—*pas* is also *not,* then
it followed therefore ergo ipso
facto inescapably that I was her
Not-Father, and we yowled at
how the homemade hat fit
so snugly.
                   And so the riff
became a theme, a quiet tether
across four decades—high school,
the English major, her marriage in
a distant state, two daughters, too
many soccer fields to count, late
night texts after the Tigers or Wildcats

got the win—a connection, like
the earth we walked on.
                    Now, as we pace
the old neighborhood, counting steps,
our paths converge on some corner
or at church or at her mother's table
on a Sunday. Or on a Hallmark card
that swims with good wishes—hers,
her husband's, the daughters', the cats'—
till *Pas-Père* rises from the crowded page,
and I know once more who I am.

Home Again

He held her pinkie as they walked,
she says. Four decades later, his heavy

steps upstairs are my rising fear
that he's lost, adrift in dark need.

He could replant the peony from Mobile,
she says, put out bulbs for daffodils

and amaryllis in spring. He'll sign with
a job service again. His bumps and knocks

above us, the hum of the shower,
tug us deeper into the flood.

Our strained voices are bubbles rising
soundless toward the light.

A Place of His Own

Thrown together when he was eight,
we had no space we could share, my
heart brimming with love for his mother,
grief for an absent son and daughter,

his own world fraught with anger
at broken promises, a gnawing need
for the father who lived elsewhere
and kept away, contempt for every rule

that hemmed him in. Four decades,
three marriages, and two children later,
he lives upstairs for months, hopping rides
to and from the quality-control job

he finally has, chafing at the ban
on beer, squeezing pay, catching up
on child support, sharing bedrooms
and bath with son and daughter on

their visits. One year in, he's keeping
pace, taking out life insurance for
the kids, nurturing the special daughter,
buying the son a used Civic, enduring

gout, scouring want ads for a place
to rent, winning custody of the son.
It is three rooms plus a narrow sunken
kitchen, a bath with cracked shower

and no sink, and one laboring window unit.
But scrubbed, aired, stocked with cast-off
sofas, beds, sheets, t.v. with no cable,
collected pots, pans, plastic dishes,

fridge packed by his mother with chicken,
pork chops, salad, fruit, it is home. He
cooks eggs, bacon for the son, goes to
football games, rides to work with

a steady friend. Is this space apart
a way for him to grow—clear the docket
and find a road he is licensed to drive on—
or have I once more shut him out?

The Eagle

Weathered, scratched, pocked, one
wing broken, gaping white plaster,
its golden sheen gone dull brown,

it is yet poised for flight—a surprise
gift from a struggling son, salvaged
from an estate sale—mascot of my

alma mater that loses routinely
to his Capstone team in the big game—
a generous gesture squeezed from

a skin-tight, night-shift budget.
We place it in a backyard corner
near the rescue hound's ashes,

beneath leaning cherry laurels and
a thriving young oak where sparrows,
redbirds, and towhees shelter and sing,

beside steady St. Francis. The eagle's
flat head and curved beak turn toward
the placid saint, an intact eye fixed

on him—alert, intent, quizzical—unsure
if this lover of creatures small and great
will take him in.

Part V: A Time to Build Up

The Royal Family

First in line, leader of the parade
of grandchildren, she loves any
sentence containing *beach,* an addict

of sun and sand before she crawled
out of diapers, beer a bonus years
later. From the speech therapy major

she leapt to a Big Easy classroom,
teaching words to third-graders, taking
wide-eyed scholars to Saints games.

Names of men float like confetti from
the south, vague, distant, as immigrant
becomes squatter, citizen. The home

tether is a rope she follows north in all
weathers—Easter, Thanksgiving, Christmas—
her voice loud on customs to be kept—

the brunch, seven-layer salad, gifts,
the bright tree with its medley of ornaments
from years past. New is the little black

and white dog whose exotic breed means
lion and whose name is a *pearl*—trotting
with head high, commanding the world,

absorbing her mistress into a routine
of food, walks, poop scooping, baths,
grooming appointments, house training.

In pet-friendly dives Maggie plays the
sleepy monarch from the bar, oblivious
to the spirited clamor of her subjects—

better behaved, Sarah says, than children
of married friends. Men are on their own,
must make a place for the little dog

with dark, steady eyes, who waits at
day's end for the tired teacher, a bundle
of barks and energy, ready to play,

fetch tossed toys, curl with her companion
on the bed, secure with the one
whose name means merely *princess*.

Actually

"So glad you dropped in to visit,"
I say to the six-year-old.
                      "Actually,"
she replies, "Mama made us." Always
one for facts, setting the record straight,
our little engineer.
                 An entrepreneur
at twelve, she presses the mayor till
he mails the license for her trade—
Nerdy Works—corralling cyber-ponies,
making them prance, cleaning clutter
from all sites.
                    Goalie
guarding the net, soccer ref knowing
all the cards, security guard keeping
the beat at raucous festivals,
                       she tames
stubborn forces from her birth, unruly
enzymes, managing the meds, tamping
panic when it rises.
                  She makes a home,
nurturing the dog, the cat, the ferret,
waving her Bernie flag, in-your-face
about justice for all, the color line,
touting the left-out, the poor, those
beyond our picket fence, outside
the flimsy boxes we file people in.

Knowing how fragile is all song, all
breath, she is tender with her special
cousin, drives the car-less uncle to work,
squeezes time for visits with grandparents
and never leaves without making clear
exactly how she feels.

Breakfast at the Beach

Over fruit and yogurt as we
watch dolphins in the surf,
my granddaughter shows me
her ultimatum to a persistent
suitor who troubled her sleep:

*stop texting me i luv u
like a friend let me go.*

Later, on the beach, she asks, "Why
do I feel like I just lost a friend?"

               ***

Five decades vanish, and Hannah
rises before me like a blue-eyed genie,
her laughter echoing across crowded rooms
at the urban school where I studied
Chaucer and Milton in weekly seminars.

She didn't shrink when we touched or
when she visited my parents' country home
or when our talk wandered into a future
we might share.   After dodging
a distant war drove me states away
to teach verbs and nouns, her phone calls
and scented letters filled my dreams
and waking thoughts.   That summer
of the thesis deadline she made a happy
space for picnics in the park where
tender feelings might take root and grow.

But the park was empty save for grackles
and stifling heat, and I begged off.

***

"Sometimes," I say to my granddaughter,
"you have to do things that make you
feel bad," waves washing our feet
as we walk, flinging up driftwood
and broken shells, life forms surviving
time out of mind.

The Call

At 7:02 the phone buzzes. I'm good,
she says. I walked Ruby Dee; we did
three laps around the neighborhood.
   The geese are out by the pond today.
I saw the heron yesterday. Grandma
didn't answer, but Auntie Rae is taking
me shopping Saturday. I got up at 5:03.
Ruby Dee was whining. I ate cereal
and a little yogurt. I weigh fifteen
pounds for today, one-five-seven-six.
   I'm on chapter 7 in *City of Ashes,* page
163. I texted Emily; she's coming to
see me Christmas. The counselors called
yesterday. I'm doing my wash; the basket
was running over. Can you get me a
wooden Indian for my birthday? Did
you get the painting I sent? It's a dragon,
and a wolf in a cave. I made a bracelet.
   I really miss Cousin Jessica. I wrote
a poem about her; it's for Aunt Roxie.
Can I type it when I get there? Can
Grandmother wrap presents for me?
Can she read *Eragon* with me? Can we
make gingerbread? I'd like soup for lunch.
   Mom gave me an emergency pill last night.
I went to bed at 5:00. Dustin texted me
every single time I tried to sleep. "Boy,
why you texting me so late?" He wants
to get married. I took a shower at 2:00
this morning, then went back to bed. Mom
said the music was too loud. How's Daddy?
How's Allie? How's Uncle Jon? I'm watching
Masked Singer. I did a rap song yesterday.

Ruby Dee scratched me; we were dancing.
   Yes, I've got my key and my book. Can I have coffee when I get there, with whipped cream?

Hands

At the self-help Admissions monitor
in the college where I taught writing
for thirty years,
                    my grandson's fingers
dart across the keyboard *first name*
last name   address   gender. At
race/ethnicity   he clicks "nonhispanic,"
pauses, then adds "black/African American."

For his slender muscular body,
the fingers are long and graceful, as if
he might play the piano or pluck soft
locks of cotton from bolls in August
heat, like Pete, Jerry, Robert, and Ralph
in my childhood.
                    In truth, his fingers
are more at home gripping a football
before he arcs it forty-plus yards
into a racing receiver's waiting hands,

or dribbling a basketball deftly into
a crowded lane, then bouncing the ball
past defenders to a lanky teammate for
a quick layup
                  or feinting a drive
from the corner, stepping back, and
lifting the spinning ball twenty feet
into the basket for three points.
                  When
he was five—in the hotel pool where
we'd gone to watch the Braves and Orioles
on a sweltering Fourth weekend—we
two played swim-as-far-as-you-can in
the pool's clear water.

                        Over and over
he pushed hard from the concrete edge,
swimming toward me under water as
I backed deeper and deeper into the pool,
his brown hand blurred in the rippling liquid,
reaching for and grasping mine again
and again, before he burst the surface,
gasped for air, and flung water to the side
with a toss of his head.
                        Now, after riding
a culture of ease and athletics through
his senior year, sleeping here, there,
at his mom's, his dad's, at this or that
grandparent's house, at a coach's or
girlfriend's house, with classes lagging
before he sprinted for two months to get to
graduation, he's ready to walk.
                        We tell him
the world is open, he can do what he will—
teaching, coaching, barbering, the military.
Before such wide space, so many choices,
he hesitates, unsure of these strange waters.

Consider Lillie

Her name's a flower that leans
toward the sun, springs new from
cold and dormant earth every year,

its fragile blooms hiding deep roots,
with petals strong and subtle as a
spider's web, orange like a crouched

tiger, steady and bright as a star.
She bikes, runs, swings a smooth
forehand, and flashes A's on every

card. The only one, she's a guarded
treasure, her quick smile gleaming;
secure enough to shake the mayor's hand

or leap with splayed limbs from the
boathouse roof into the lake.
                                      In her

firming features—the darkening
auburn hair—I see her Mimi's face,
and in her tall stature, I see my own.

May she grow the best of all of us—
a house bright and solid as the Lego
village she built in childhood—an open

heart never bruised, that in giving
returns a hundredfold, grace rising
like piano notes through all her days—

love and joy rooted deep through all
weathers, as sure as the lily blooming
fresh every spring.

Jonah

< Heb, *a dove*

Amid the chatter and clatter of family
dinner, birthday wishes tossed across
the table, homemade cheesecake, raucous
singing, and the glare of seventy-five
candles,
        the sturdy blond boy who speaks
beyond his seven years asks the old man,
"What are your goals for next year?" as if
someone so far in would surely have a plan.

The plan is to know the boy, how as a tot
he threw the plastic ball, then the baseball,
strong and true, how with bat cocked and
steady eye he swung and smacked the ball,
how he caught the throw in the tip of the glove
and yowled at his ice-cream-cone catch.

How he pushes a skateboard with grace
and speed around the park's perimeter till
at the far turn his tow head bobs in and out
of view like a darting bird in flight.
                              How
like the dove, he sometimes mourns, when
a phone game gets shut down or when the
the six-inch bass that struck his fly and bit
has to be dropped back into the lake,
                              how
like the dove he loves peace—for all his
karate kicks and twists, going soft on a
smaller foe, quicker to defend than bash.

How he fell for words and stories in the
cradle, screaming through tears in time-out,
"I want a book!" catching the lilt and beat
and crisp edges of adult language long before
he grasped the logic,
                                      reading
to his kindergarten class, vaulting so high
on the trampoline that he flipped in mid-air
and landed squarely in second grade, already
tall as the older boys.
                            How, sitting still
on the sofa, spell-bound, oblivious to every
clock, leaning toward the page, he enters
the book's spacious world, inhales phrases
that help him weasel through loopholes,
deflect a directive to take out the garbage
or get dressed, phrases that gain him freedom,
screen time, and move him to interrogate

his beaming grandfather, who—a lover of
phrases himself—must surely have an answer.

Sophie

< Gr *sophia,* wisdom, skill

"Wisdom cries out in the street; in the squares she raises her voice."
—Proverbs 1:20, NRSV

Who knew wisdom was a blue-eyed blonde
six-year-old?
                     If she cries out in the street,
it's because her speeding bike, zipping around
the empty circle on Lennox Loop weaving
figure-eights, banking across slanted driveways,
skidding to a stop inches short of the garage door,
slid out when she took a curve too fast, grinding
a knee on the gritty pavement—till she's up
and off again.
                     Or because her deft
fingers reaching for raspberries in thick, thorny
foliage strikes a sharp stem—and she pauses
before plopping another berry between
smiling red-stained lips.
                     Or because the limp
cat she hauls about the house, its tail dragging,
stiffens and leaps to freedom, raking a forearm
till she rubs it and laughs at the loss.
                     Or
because the chattering family in the van ignore
her strains of "My bonnie lies over the ocean"
from the far back seat.
                     Or because bouncing
rhythmically higher and higher on the trampoline
she flips and crashes on a shoulder.
                     Or—
stranded atop the tall backyard maple or sitting
among scattered pieces of a large puzzle on the

hardwood floor or crowded to a corner while
her brother does karate demo twists and kicks—
she cries out because the world won't watch her
prove that whatever moves and jumps and turns
her brother can do, she can do just as well.

Part VI: A Time to Dance

GP's Wife Does National Boards

So what's the plan, she says, tapping
a fingernail on her coffee cup, marching
through pages of morning news as I
study high school football scores;
do you have goals, objectives, strategy,
a mission, and are you effective?

> Her skin is soft, I know, and cool
> like swamp oak shade, rich as
> ploughed ground in springtime.

We could move this wall twelve feet,
she adds, open the sunroom, put the pool
by the fence, plant azaleas, and grow
Eden out back; while I, bursting joy's
week-old grapes, note Goshen lost,
Reeltown beat Beulah, and Leroy is undefeated.

> Her hands are finely formed and sure,
> true as tall pine, light as evening
> breeze across a summer porch.

Flicking crumbs, I clip play-off grids,
tasting pleasure for weeks to come.
Next term, she says, I'm teaching part-time
at two colleges, chairing my department,
doing National Boards, becoming president
of City Educators, and taking the girls abroad.
What do you plan to do?

> Beside her tapping foot, arched and brown
> with beach-front sun, our fattened cat
> lies twitching in his dream.

As You Like It
or
GP Goes to London with His Wife

We've crossed the sea to honor
silver years of married bliss, a score
and more of passion, romance, children, work,
houses, hunger, taxes, graduate school, ex-spouses,
and a thousand other shocks borne together.
We've grown the knack for space, the several
tracks we run, teaching, going out
with the guys, a model of modern blending,
his and hers finely tuned.

Sweet Thames, run softly
Till I end my song.

But on Millenium Bridge, in the city
Romans ruled twenty centuries past,
we argue over pictures. Behind us,
Milton's bones rest in St. Giles, Keats's
Elgin marbles pose in broken grandeur, and
the dome of St. Paul's looms like a god
above busy streets, fire, plague, and smoke.
Before us, the New Globe rises
from cold ashes, mortal lovers
play the fool, and Juliet sleeps,
waiting for her Romeo.

Sweet Thames, run softly
While I make my moan.

You're in charge of photos, she says,
thrusting me the large Minolta Maxxum
bristling with buttons and lenses

to take our happy time.
I didn't do the course, I reply,
holding up my borrowed Canon One-Shot,
I want to look, not fumble. And so
while nations come and go,
she pushes and I deny, frozen
in history, reeking of righteous anger
at this betrayal of the tender art
of connubial compromise. In the Bard's new home,
we take our separate shots
of beams and stage and open sky, and Rosalind
conning lines that love is madness.

Sweet Thames, run softly
Till I end my song.

In the Millenium Hotel, spooned snug
and warm beneath duvet, we dream
oceans bear us home beneath a thousand stars,
singing Hymen, god of every town.

Darwin Chuckles
or
GP Studies Natural Selection

She does early church, cooks peas,
okra, spareribs, fried potatoes, beaming
as her children, grandkids, mother,
husband pile their plates, poring over
recipes for next week's feast, buying
cookbooks for gifts.

                                    Meanwhile, he retires, runs
                     the park in dripping heat, eats apples,
                     yogurt, solves sodokus and cryptoquotes,
                     devouring books like English muffins,
                     weighing every morning.

She joins Weight Watchers, Curves, a local gym,
walks with a friend at school, tries Atkins,
tuna fish, drinks fat-free cream, and buys
new robes as sizes grow.

                              He plays the granddad,
                     watching girls at soccer, throws the football
                     in the yard, sending Nathan deep or down
                     and out for the perfect spiral, jogging from
                     the field to roars of hometown crowds.

She goes out with the girls,
laughing over sagging body parts
and birthday cards where women cash in
sex for cake, sighing that their ageing husbands
always ask for more.

                    Over lunch with friends,
            he comments on an ample cleavage, bare
            tanned midriff tight as a trampoline. He
            scrubs pots, washes clothes, mops, changes
            out the vacuum bag, cuts the yard, digs
            for family roots, and sings alone in church.

Taking pills to keep her pressure down, she
teaches hordes, marking papers every night,
munching chips, sipping brandy, fingering
her laptop. She reads the *Ya-Ya* books in bed,
worries that a son will drink or overspend,
a grandson won't make the gifted class, that
she should see sick friends, sucking into orbit
every wandering satellite.

                            He spills himself
            in poems, sending them around to cousins
            and old students, hot to see his name
            in print. Hugging women that he meets, he
            knows full well Victoria's Secret and
            swimsuit models' names, feeding desire
            as if it were an old dog that might starve.

About Time

She points proudly to all the dates
on her calendar—Clothes Closet at 8:00,
Mama at noon, dentist at 2:00, vestry
at 5:00 with drinks afterwards—a work
of art merging refrigerator notes, her phone,
husband's desk scrawlings, grandchildren's
baseball games, visits of grown children,
wedding invitations and travel plans,
the world reduced to bare action
yet to happen, with no surprises, like
horses in the starter's gate poised, ready,
and curbed till she says go.

He likes nothing so much as a blank page,
time as unexplored space, the morning
undefined, with coffee, a redbird's whistle,
yesterday's news, his thoughts, a yellow rose
defiant in the parched flower bed. His list,
scattered across three rooms on torn bits
of scratch paper, is largely unsequenced—
answer e-mails, submit poems, cut grass,
pick up London photos, run in park, schedule
trip to Colorado—inroads and byways
of possibility jarred only by the thunder
of approaching hooves.

Probably Not
or
The Tangled Art of Connubial Meta-Messages

If he said a simple question like,
    "What time is it?" deserves
        a simple answer, not an angled comment
            like, "You can finish that poem tomorrow,"

If she knew that he, a second child,
    always craved to please
        and writhed under criticism
            like cornstalks in a drought,

If he explained that
    as a chubby boy he learned
        the game of making women like him
            and never found a way to stop,

If she knew that budget overruns
    ticked him off and he admitted
        he hadn't after all forgiven her
            the pounds she gained on happy pills,

Would she understand why he asked if
    the dog had peed, and when she snapped that
        dogfood costs less than running shoes, why he
            yelled, "Goddammit! All I want is
        a straight answer!"?

Would she agree that
    dancing before funhouse mirrors
        saves all the kisses of youth and
            lays balm on deepest wounds?

Absence

Alarmed at how he missed her, how
fingers fell from the hand that had

touched her face, arms dropped off
that once reached to hold her, a leg

vanished that felt her warmth in bed, lips
numb that brushed hers as she left, ears

dead that listened for her call—alarmed,
he spoke curtly when she returned, words

edged in cool politeness, eyes pleading
to be whole again.

An Evening

On a Saturday, they have steak
picked up at Lucky's Meat Market,
her thick filet seared two minutes
on each side, leaving it red, juicy,
his given an added turn, tender,
a paler red. These are trimmed
with new potatoes slathered with
butter and sour cream, and spinach
salad tossed in homemade blue cheese.

Trays on knees, in chairs shaped
by years to their contours, they
click glasses of Pinot as she pulls up
the DVR list of recordings for *Blacklist,
Scandal, Law and Order,* and the wild
intrigues of *Grey's Anatomy.*

This Only

"The awful daring of a moment's surrender
Which an age of prudence can never retract
By this, and this only, have we existed."
        —T.S. Eliot, *The Waste Land*

As he enters her, feeling
the ancient warmth rich

with promise, he knows
for the barest instant

what he wants most
is to be inside

her deepest self,
the place where

nothing happens, where
being is enough.

There he would sit with her,
touch her hand, laugh

at all their folly, pull
her to him while rain

lashed the window.
Afterwards, he is

astonished that the dog
curls in her bed,

the microwave clock
still counts their time,

and the coffee pot
steams half full.

Aiding and Abetting

Small and white, not blue—and dear
as mortgage payments—the pills are

splints to get him through the dance,
a cane to lean on, staff for support

as they climb the slope. But the music
fades, as does his breath. All's not well

that begins well. He remembers a catch
he made in left center, running full speed.

He felt he could shag anything. Her
fingertips awaken him, and they lean in,

move together through need, desire,
muscle memory, sore knees, shuffling

toward some final note they find
satisfactory.

Part VII: A Time for Peace

Packing Up

for Georgia Crumbley, 1921-2018

Throughout the house, under primal dust—
we find Christmas and birthday cards, bank statements,
half-used lipstick tubes, perfume bottles, old
dresses, shoes, hats, purses, magazines she
thought she might use again, tax records,
cake mixes and canned goods long out of date,
three sewing machines, four vacuum cleaners,
a phonograph from the fifties, Ball jars
and lids, yellowed newspaper clippings
saying someone died or won a prize, receipts
for water and electricity month after month,
for roofing and nails after the tornado came,
hospital bills for back surgery, three
generations of dolls, toy tractors, plastic
army men that children and grandchildren
have outgrown, quilting scraps, quilt tops,
batting for quilts, dozens of letters
from Aunt Jessie, an entire filing cabinet
of Sunday school lessons, a ponderous set
of World Books describing life before Sputnik,
pictures of children as babies, of the late
husband shirtless, relaxed after work.

At ninety-five she moves
into neat new living quarters, with
sitting room, bedroom, cozy kitchen,
and we are left to sift, toss, shred,
store in one sturdy trunk what makes
the cut—packing, tucking, smoothing,
till all that remains fits firmly in the box.

All Things New

*"This seeing the sick endears them to us,
us, too, it endears."*
—Hopkins, "Felix Randall"

Twenty-three days after her mother dies
of heart failure at 97, my wife lies still,
sedated, as a surgeon slices open her right
anterior hip, somehow through blood
saws the ball off the femur, drives with
hammer strokes a titanium rod with new
ball into the top of the bone, inserts
a new socket into the pelvis so that
bone and metal will grow as one, then
closes the six-inch incision with twenty-one
staples. This is the inflamed and crumbling
joint that has hurt for three years—with
no time for wife-daughter-grandmother
to pause for new parts.

                    The same day,
numb on Narco, she walks room and hall
and next day goes home, laughing that she
is her mother pushing a walker, leaning
left on the worn cane.

                    Under a flood of nausea
driven by meds, anemia, systemic outrage,
pounds collapse, erode like beach castles,
arms shrink, voice goes weak, eyes dark
and hollow. She who took care must now
be cared for, a general making requests
from her infirmary bed—pills, a pillow,
decaf mocha from Java Jaay, fast food
wake-up wrap of eggs and cheese, all
the palate can endure.

                    Three weeks after
the last opiates and into teeth-gritting Tylenol,
she showers on her own, gets breakfast,
is dropped at a friend's for lunch, has her
toenails done, takes dinner at a restaurant.
Doing therapy like clockwork, she walks
up and down steps, kicks forward, back,
to the side, sits, rises; at the kitchen sink
marches firmly in place toward Gulf Shores,
Idaho, Vienna, Prague, a backlog of venues
we relish in the breakfast nook over roasted
peppers, fried chicken, and beef soup she made,
passing the Sunday crossword back and forth.

In the flower bed outside the window, newly
set coneflowers, tick seed, daisies, impatiens
bloom a lush medley of crimson, orange,
white, lavender, and brilliant yellow.

To Your Health

> < *OE hal*, sound, healthy, whole

Eight weeks in—after I hooked a toe
on a jutting sidewalk corner by the Palers',
plunged forward, and cracked a carpal

in the wrist—the bone has *healed,* snaked
fibers across the gap, meshed, solidified,
and is now *whole,* so that I can flex, grip,

lift, push again, no longer broken, partial,
once more *hale* if not hearty.
                            As did

the flesh on my forearm after the bent
crepe myrtle limb I was sawing sprang
like a metal trap and dug a two-inch gash

beneath the papery skin, the E.R. doctor
smiling as she pulled together the two
ragged sides and sutured them, so that

cells connected, bonded, sealed the wound
that is now a pale scar across a bulging
blue vein. We crave to be one, not parts,

pieces, shards, to have *health.* We hurt
when skin, bones, homes, friendships,
marriages break, when the heart

fractures, pieces jarred apart, till hands
connect across a chasm, and we are one
again. *Hail* to the body's relentless drive

to mend, contain, keep together both
its ageing self and its reckless tenant,
the abstracted and clumsy spirit.

A Way Forward

for Daisy

Language is the path we hack
through bushes, briers, vines, saplings,
burgeoning undergrowth till we walk
without thought beneath thick and
towering mystery,
                           steering
the rescue hound along Gordon Drive
under a leaning hackberry, two tall
willow oaks dropping decayed limbs
in wind and rain,
                    beside the woodpecker-
riddled pecan whose base the dog
sniffs, sorting squirrels, ground-feeding
flickers, other dogs hiking a leg or
squatting—her own medley of forms that
will move her when she lies twitching,
half-barking in her dream.
                          She smells
the brush pile on 10th, dying leaves, twigs,
pine boughs tossed to clear a way for
the neat wooden fence blocking our
view into the yard.
                  Padding the beaten
sidewalk toward home, we greet other dogs,
other walkers, lamenting, with a neighbor,
the bulldog's untimely demise.
                    Far ahead,
where the street stretches, narrows, ends,
cars climb northward on the river bridge,
to a world beyond the hound's gray muzzle
and steady panting, beyond my graying

temples and aching knee—rich with wide
water and sky, birds, trees, foxes—a world
we have not named.

Sure Thing

< L *securus* < *se*, free from
+ *cura*, care

All is pending, provisional, tentative,
the ham and cheese with mustard
and sliced dill for lunch,
                         steady
spasms of the heart, dogs barking,
sirens keening in the distance,

a waning gibbous moon above
the Pucketts' house at 5:00 a.m.
as I go for the morning paper,

the son's "Hey, Dad" across a
continent as he drives to work
and says Idaho is cold with
slushy snow,
                   the wife's hand
reaching for mine at 3:00 a.m.
under covers.
                 All hangs by a tether,
clutched, savored, till it drops away
and the cosmos sighs, smooths itself,

like a wrinkle on the lap of an apron,
a ripple across a still pond at twilight.

About the Author

Recipient of the 2014 Writers Exchange Award from Poets & Writers, **Harry Moore** is the author of the poetry collection *Bearing the Farm Away* (Kelsay Books, 2018) and four chapbooks: *What He Would Call Them* (Finishing Line Press, 2013); *Time's Fool: Love Poems* (Mule on a Ferris Wheel Press, Huntsville, AL, 2014); *Retreat: A Way Forward* (Finishing Line Press, 2017); and *Beyond Paradise: The Unweeded Garden* (Main Street Rag, 2020).

His poems have appeared or are forthcoming in *Sow's Ear Poetry Review, Plainsongs, Xavier Review, Pudding Magazine, Main Street Rag, South Carolina Review, Blue Unicorn, Slipstream, Anglican Theological Review, Ponder Review,* and other journals.

Retired after teaching writing and literature for four decades in Alabama community colleges, he currently lives with his wife, Cassandra, in Decatur, Alabama, and serves as an assistant editor of *POEM* magazine.

Visit the author's web site at: harryvmoore.com.

www.ingramcontent.com/pod-product-compliance
Lightning Source LLC
Chambersburg PA
CBHW070512090426
42735CB00012B/2747